# Sauces & Dips

**40 DELICIOUS CLASSIC AND CONTEMPORARY RECIPES**

# Sauces & Dips

## 40 DELICIOUS CLASSIC AND CONTEMPORARY RECIPES

Marks and Spencer p.l.c.
PO Box 3339
Chester CH99 9QS
www.marksandspencer.com
T40/8284/0259

ISBN: 1-84461-593-6

Printed in Italy

Design concept by Mark Roberts (Talking Design)

**Notes for the Reader**
This book uses both metric and imperial measurements. Follow the same
units of measurement throughout; do not mix metric and imperial. All spoon
measurements are level: teaspoons are assumed to be 5 ml, and tablespoons
are assumed to be 15 ml. Unless otherwise stated, milk is assumed to be full
fat, eggs and individual vegetables such as potatoes are medium and pepper
is freshly ground black pepper. Recipes using raw or very lightly cooked eggs
should be avoided by infants, the elderly, pregnant women, convalescents and
anyone suffering from an illness. The times given are an approximate guide only.

**Picture acknowledgement**
The Bridgewater Book Company Ltd would like to thank Joanna McCarthy/Iconica/
Getty Images for permission to reproduce copyright material for the endpapers.

# Contents

# Introduction

It is said that one of the things that distinguishes a good cook from a great one is the quality of their sauces. A sauce can spice things up, add creamy richness, enhance the flavour of a dish's main ingredient, and often adds a touch of elegance to the presentation.

The dividing line between sauces and dips is a narrow one and there are numerous recipes that span it. In this book, the section of recipes classified as dips includes all those delicious snacks and canapés that can be served with crudités, pitta bread, breadsticks and so on to make a single, stand-alone dish. Nevertheless, many can also serve as sauces. Try Guacamole with grilled steak, Hummus with braised lamb or Pico de Gallo Salsa with barbecued chicken, for example.

Three further sections are devoted exclusively to sauces in the conventional sense. Savoury Sauces includes many worldwide favourites that can make or break a recipe. Just try to imagine crisp little fish cakes without Thai Dipping Sauce or succulent steamed asparagus without Hollandaise. This book provides a collection of sauces and salad dressings that form the core of a cook's repertoire. These range from such traditional standbys as Mayonnaise to more contemporary accompaniments such as Mango Chutney and Apricot Sauce. Finally, Sweet Sauces offers a host of alternatives to the ubiquitous custard or whipped cream, including, of course, some special treats for chocoholics.

# Delicious Dips

Whether you serve them with a colourful platter of raw vegetables or a basket of sesame seed crackers, dips are the key to easy entertaining. With 18 recipes, and ingredients as varied as avocados, beans, red peppers and coconut here, there will be something to suit every taste and every budget. This is a truly international collection, with dishes from countries as far apart as Mexico, Indonesia, Greece and India and with flavours ranging from hot and spicy to cool and refreshing, from rich and creamy to sharp and tantalizing. As they are all so easy to make, you can serve a whole array of dips as part of a party buffet table. Equally, two or three contrasting dips would make an unusual starter for a dinner party and get the taste buds tingling and the conversation rolling. You can even serve individual dips as a colourful and attractive accompaniment to liven up a simple main course.

# Guacamole

**SERVES** 4

2 LARGE, RIPE AVOCADOS

JUICE OF 1 LIME, OR TO TASTE

2 TSP OLIVE OIL

$1/2$ ONION, FINELY CHOPPED

1 FRESH GREEN CHILLI, SUCH AS POBLANO, DESEEDED AND FINELY CHOPPED

1 GARLIC CLOVE, CRUSHED

$1/4$ TSP GROUND CUMIN

1 TBSP CHOPPED FRESH CORIANDER

SALT AND PEPPER

CHOPPED FRESH CORIANDER, TO GARNISH

Cut the avocados in half lengthways and twist the 2 halves in opposite directions to separate. Stab the stone with the point of a sharp knife and lift out.

Peel, then roughly chop the avocado halves and place in a non-metallic bowl. Squeeze over the lime juice and add the oil.

Mash the avocados with a fork until the desired consistency is reached – either chunky or smooth. Blend in the onion, chilli, garlic, cumin and chopped coriander, then season to taste with salt and pepper.

Transfer to a serving dish and serve immediately, to avoid discoloration. Sprinkle with extra chopped coriander, if liked.

*There are as many versions of this dish as there are cooks, but a good result always depends on using quality, ripe avocados. Mashing rather than puréeing gives control over the texture.*

# Hummus

225 G/8 OZ CHICKPEAS,
COVERED WITH WATER AND
SOAKED OVERNIGHT

JUICE OF 2 LARGE LEMONS

150 ML/¼ PINT TAHINI

2 GARLIC CLOVES, CRUSHED

4 TBSP EXTRA-VIRGIN OLIVE OIL

SMALL PINCH OF GROUND CUMIN

SALT AND PEPPER

1 TSP PAPRIKA

FLAT-LEAF PARSLEY, CHOPPED,
TO GARNISH

WARM PITTA BREAD, TO SERVE

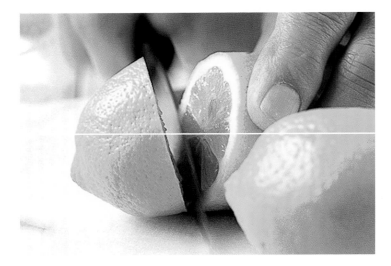

*This is a favourite dish frequently served in Greek restaurants. It has an earthy flavour and, although it can be bought, the flavour of the home-made variety is much better. It is improved if made with dried, as opposed to canned, chickpeas. Fortunately it is simple to make, especially if prepared in a food processor.*

If using dried chickpeas that have soaked overnight, drain, put in a saucepan and cover with cold water. Bring to the boil, then simmer for about 2 hours, until very tender.

Drain the chickpeas, reserving a little of the liquid, and put in a food processor, reserving a few to garnish. Blend the chickpeas until smooth, gradually adding the lemon juice and enough reserved liquid to form a smooth, thick purée. Add the tahini, garlic, 3 tablespoons of the olive oil and the cumin and blend until smooth. Season with salt and pepper.

Turn the mixture into a shallow serving dish and chill in the refrigerator for 2–3 hours before serving. To serve, mix the reserved olive oil with the paprika and drizzle over the top of the dish. Sprinkle with the parsley and the reserved chickpeas. Accompany with warm pitta bread.

# Heavenly Garlic Dip

**SERVES 4**

2 BULBS GARLIC

6 TBSP OLIVE OIL

1 SMALL ONION, FINELY CHOPPED

2 TBSP LEMON JUICE

3 TBSP TAHINI

2 TBSP CHOPPED FRESH PARSLEY

SALT AND PEPPER

FRESH VEGETABLE CRUDITÉS,
TO SERVE

FRENCH BREAD OR WARM PITTA
BREADS, TO SERVE

Separate the bulbs of garlic into individual cloves. Place them on a baking tray and roast in a preheated oven, 200°C/400°F/Gas Mark 6, for 8–10 minutes. Set them aside to cool for a few minutes.

When they are cool enough to handle, peel the garlic cloves and then chop them finely.

Heat the olive oil in a saucepan or frying pan and add the garlic and onion. Fry over a low heat, stirring occasionally, for 8–10 minutes, until softened. Remove the pan from the heat.

Mix in the lemon juice, tahini and parsley. Season to taste with salt and pepper. Transfer the dip to a small heatproof bowl.

Serve with fresh vegetable crudités, or with chunks of French bread or warm pitta breads.

*If you come across smoked garlic, use it in this recipe – it tastes wonderful. There is no need to roast the smoked garlic, so omit the first step.*

# Tzatziki

SERVES 4

1 SMALL CUCUMBER

300 ML/$\frac{1}{2}$ PINT AUTHENTIC
GREEK YOGURT

1 LARGE GARLIC CLOVE, CRUSHED

1 TBSP CHOPPED FRESH
MINT OR DILL

SALT AND PEPPER

WARM PITTA BREAD, TO SERVE

Peel, then coarsely grate the cucumber. Put in a sieve and squeeze out as much of the water as possible. Put the cucumber into a bowl.

Add the yogurt, garlic and chopped mint (reserve a little as a garnish, if liked) to the cucumber and season with pepper. Mix well together and chill in the refrigerator for about 2 hours before serving.

To serve, stir the cucumber and yogurt dip and transfer to a serving bowl. Sprinkle with salt and accompany with warm pitta bread.

*This wonderfully cooling combination of yogurt, cucumber and mint is especially good as an accompaniment to very spicy curries. If you are taken by surprise with the heat of a curry, don't reach for a glass of water – instead, try this soothing dip!*

# Aïoli

SERVES 4

3 LARGE GARLIC CLOVES, FINELY CHOPPED

2 EGG YOLKS

225 ML/8 FL OZ EXTRA-VIRGIN OLIVE OIL

1 TBSP LEMON JUICE

1 TBSP LIME JUICE

1 TBSP DIJON MUSTARD

1 TBSP CHOPPED FRESH TARRAGON

SALT AND PEPPER

1 FRESH TARRAGON SPRIG, TO GARNISH

Ensure that all the ingredients are at room temperature. Place the garlic and egg yolks in a food processor and process until well blended. With the motor running, pour in the oil, teaspoon by teaspoon, through the feeder tube until the mixture starts to thicken, then pour in the remaining oil in a thin stream until a thick mayonnaise forms.

Add the lemon and lime juices, mustard and tarragon and season to taste with salt and pepper. Blend the mixture until smooth, then transfer to a non-metallic bowl. Cover with clingfilm and refrigerate until required. Garnish with a tarragon sprig.

*It is essential to add oil slowly to the egg yolks, until between one-third and one-half has been fully incorporated, to prevent the mixture from curdling. If the mixture does curdle, add it, a little at a time, to another egg yolk, whisking constantly, then return it to the food processor, with the motor running, and gradually add the remaining oil.*

# Taramasaláta

SERVES 6

225 G/8 OZ SMOKED COD ROE
OR FRESH GREY MULLET ROE

1 SMALL ONION, ROUGHLY
CHOPPED

55 G/2 OZ FRESH WHITE
BREADCRUMBS

1 LARGE GARLIC CLOVE, CRUSHED

GRATED RIND AND JUICE OF
1 LARGE LEMON

150 ML/¼ PINT EXTRA-VIRGIN
OLIVE OIL

6 TBSP HOT WATER

PEPPER

CRACKERS, POTATO CRISPS OR
PITTA BREAD, TO SERVE

*To Garnish*

SLICED BLACK GREEK OLIVES

SLICED CAPERS

CHOPPED FLAT-LEAF PARSLEY

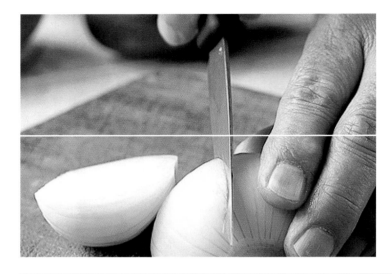

*This dish was traditionally made with salted mullet roe, which is the true tarama and from which it derives its Greek name taramasaláta. Nowadays, however, it is usually made with smoked cod roe, which is more readily available.*

Remove the skin from the fish roe. Put the onion in a food processor and chop finely. Add the cod roe in small pieces and blend until smooth. Add the breadcrumbs, garlic, lemon rind and juice, and mix well together.

With the machine running, very slowly pour in the oil. When all the oil has been added, blend in the water. Season with pepper.

Turn the mixture into a serving bowl and chill in the refrigerator for at least 1 hour before serving. Serve garnished with olives, capers and chopped parsley and accompany with crackers, crisps or pitta bread.

# Aubergine and Pepper Dip

SERVES 6–8

2 LARGE AUBERGINES

2 RED PEPPERS

4 TBSP SPANISH OLIVE OIL

2 GARLIC CLOVES, ROUGHLY CHOPPED

GRATED RIND AND JUICE OF 1/2 LEMON

1 TBSP CHOPPED FRESH CORIANDER

1/2–1 TSP PAPRIKA

SALT AND PEPPER

FRESH CHOPPED CORIANDER, TO GARNISH

BREAD OR TOAST, TO SERVE

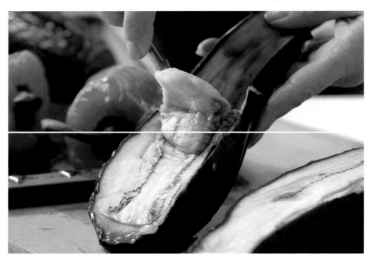

*As a variation, instead of cooking the aubergines and peppers in the oven, you can cook them under a preheated grill until the skins are charred all over. They do, however, need to be turned frequently for about 10 minutes.*

Preheat the oven to 190°C/375°F/Gas Mark 5. Prick the skins of the aubergines and peppers all over with a fork and brush with 1 tablespoon of the olive oil. Place on a baking tray and bake in the oven for 45 minutes, or until the skins are beginning to turn black, the flesh of the aubergine is very soft and the peppers are deflated.

When the vegetables are cooked, put them in a bowl and cover tightly with a clean, damp tea towel. Alternatively, you can put the cooked vegetables in a polythene bag. Leave for about 15 minutes, or until they are cool enough to handle.

When the vegetables have cooled, cut the aubergines in half lengthways, carefully scoop out the flesh and discard the skin. Cut the aubergine flesh into large chunks. Remove and discard the stem, core and seeds from the peppers and cut the flesh into large pieces.

Heat the remaining olive oil in a frying pan. Add the aubergine and pepper and fry for 5 minutes. Add the garlic and fry for a further 30 seconds.

Turn the contents of the frying pan onto kitchen paper to drain, then transfer to a food processor. Add the lemon rind and juice, the chopped coriander, the paprika, and salt and pepper to taste, then process until a speckled purée is formed.

Turn the aubergine and pepper dip into a serving bowl. Serve warm, at room temperature, or leave to cool for 30 minutes, then leave to chill in the refrigerator for at least 1 hour and serve cold. Garnish with coriander sprigs and accompany with thick slices of bread or toast for dipping.

# Tamarind Chutney

MAKES ABOUT 250 G/9 OZ

100 G/3½ OZ TAMARIND PULP, CHOPPED, OR PASTE*

450 ML/16 FL OZ WATER

½ FRESH BIRD'S EYE CHILLI, OR TO TASTE, DESEEDED AND CHOPPED

55 G/2 OZ SOFT LIGHT BROWN SUGAR, OR TO TASTE

½ TSP SALT

*READY-TO-USE TAMARIND PASTE IS AVAILABLE FROM SUPERMARKETS

*There isn't any mistaking the fresh, sour taste of tamarind; it adds a distinctive flavour to many dishes, especially those from Southern India. More like a sauce than a thick chutney, this sweet-and-sour tasting mixture is excellent served with vegetable samosas.*

Put the tamarind and water in a heavy-based saucepan over a high heat and bring to the boil. Reduce the heat to the lowest setting and simmer for 25 minutes, stirring occasionally to break up the tamarind pulp, or until tender.

Tip the tamarind pulp into a sieve and use a wooden spoon to push the pulp into the rinsed-out pan.

Stir in the chilli, sugar and salt and continue simmering for a further 10 minutes or until the desired consistency is reached. Leave to cool slightly, then stir in extra sugar or salt, according to taste.

Leave to cool completely, then cover tightly and chill for up to 3 days, or freeze.

# Mole Verde

**SERVES 4**

250 G/9 OZ TOASTED
PUMPKIN SEEDS

1 LITRE/1¾ PINTS
VEGETABLE STOCK

SEVERAL PINCHES
OF GROUND CLOVES

8–10 TOMATILLOS, DICED,
OR 225 ML/8 FL OZ MILD
TOMATILLO SALSA

½ ONION, CHOPPED

½ FRESH GREEN CHILLI,
DESEEDED AND DICED

3 GARLIC CLOVES, CHOPPED

½ TSP FRESH THYME LEAVES

½ TSP FRESH MARJORAM LEAVES

3 TBSP VEGETABLE OIL

3 BAY LEAVES

4 TBSP CHOPPED FRESH
CORIANDER

SALT AND PEPPER

Grind the toasted pumpkin seeds in a food processor. Add half the vegetable stock, the cloves, tomatillos, onion, chilli, garlic, thyme and marjoram, and blend to a purée.

Heat the vegetable oil in a heavy-based frying pan and add the puréed pumpkin seed mixture, together with the bay leaves. Cook over a medium-high heat for about 5 minutes until the mixture has begun to thicken.

Remove from the heat and add the rest of the vegetable stock and the coriander. Return the pan to the heat and cook until the sauce thickens, then remove from the heat.

Remove the bay leaves and process the sauce until completely smooth again. Add salt and pepper to taste. Transfer the sauce to a bowl and serve.

*'Moles' are Mexican purées and, depending on the ingredients, they vary in colour from yellow and green to chocolate brown. This mole is a speciality of Jalisco.*

# Chilli and Onion Chutney

1–2 FRESH GREEN CHILLIES, DESEEDED OR NOT, TO TASTE, AND FINELY CHOPPED

1 SMALL FRESH BIRD'S EYE CHILLI, DESEEDED OR NOT, TO TASTE, AND FINELY CHOPPED

1 TBSP WHITE WINE OR CIDER VINEGAR

2 ONIONS, FINELY CHOPPED

2 TBSP FRESH LEMON JUICE

1 TBSP SUGAR

3 TBSP CHOPPED FRESH CORIANDER, MINT OR PARSLEY, OR A COMBINATION OF HERBS

SALT

CHILLI FLOWER, TO GARNISH

Put the chillies in a small non-metallic bowl with the vinegar, stir and then drain. Return the chillies to the bowl and stir in the onions, lemon juice, sugar and herbs, then add salt to taste.

Leave to stand at room temperature or cover and chill for 15 minutes. Garnish with the chilli flower before serving.

*For a chilli and onion raita, stir 300 ml/10 fl oz natural yogurt into the chutney mixture and chill for at least 1 hour. Stir before serving and sprinkle with fresh herbs.*

# Coriander Chutney

**MAKES ABOUT 225 G/8 OZ**

1¹/₂ TBSP LEMON JUICE

1¹/₂ TBSP WATER

85 G/3 OZ FRESH CORIANDER
LEAVES AND STEMS, COARSELY
CHOPPED

2 TBSP CHOPPED FRESH COCONUT

1 SMALL SHALLOT,
VERY FINELY CHOPPED

5-MM/¹/₄-INCH PIECE OF
FRESH ROOT GINGER, CHOPPED

1 FRESH GREEN CHILLI,
DESEEDED AND CHOPPED

¹/₂ TSP SUGAR

¹/₂ TSP SALT

PINCH OF PEPPER

*This is an example of one of the many uncooked, fresh-tasting chutneys that are served throughout the day in India with meals or snacks.*

Put the lemon juice and water in a small food processor, add half the coriander and whiz until it is blended and a slushy paste forms. Gradually add the remaining coriander and whiz until it is all blended, scraping down the sides of the processor, if necessary. If you don't have a processor that will cope with this small amount, use a pestle and mortar, adding the coriander in small amounts.

Add the remaining ingredients and continue whizzing until they are all finely chopped and blended. Taste and adjust any of the seasonings, if you like. Transfer to a non-metallic bowl, cover and chill for up to 3 days before serving.

# Split Pea Dip

SERVES 6

250 G/9 OZ YELLOW SPLIT PEAS

2 SMALL ONIONS, 1 CHOPPED
ROUGHLY AND 1 CHOPPED
VERY FINELY

1 GARLIC CLOVE, CHOPPED
ROUGHLY

6 TBSP EXTRA-VIRGIN OLIVE OIL

1 TBSP CHOPPED FRESH OREGANO

SALT AND PEPPER

SAVOURY BISCUITS, TO SERVE

Rinse the split peas under cold running water. Put in a saucepan and add the roughly chopped onion, the garlic and plenty of cold water. Bring to the boil then simmer for about 45 minutes, until very tender.

Drain the split peas, reserving a little of the cooking liquid, and put in a food processor. Add 5 tablespoons of the olive oil and blend until smooth. If the mixture seems too dry, add enough of the reserved liquid to form a smooth, thick purée. Add the oregano and season with salt and pepper.

Turn the mixture into a serving bowl and sprinkle with the finely chopped onion and extra oregano if liked. Drizzle over the remaining olive oil. Serve warm or cold with savoury biscuits.

*This very popular Greek dish is similar to hummus, but made with yellow split peas. It is simple to make but is even easier if prepared in a food processor.*

# Aubergine and Garlic Dip

**SERVES 6**

2 LARGE AUBERGINES

50 ML/2 FL OZ EXTRA-VIRGIN OLIVE OIL

JUICE OF 1/2 LEMON

150 ML/1/4 PINT AUTHENTIC GREEK YOGURT

2 GARLIC CLOVES, CRUSHED

PINCH OF GROUND CUMIN

SALT AND PEPPER

CHOPPED FRESH FLAT-LEAF PARSLEY, TO GARNISH

STRIPS OF RED AND GREEN PEPPER, TO SERVE

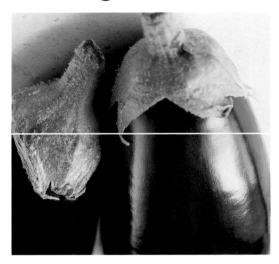 

Prick the skins of the aubergines with a fork and put on a baking tray. Bake in a preheated oven, 190°C/370°F/Gas Mark 5, for 45 minutes, or until very soft. Leave to cool slightly, then cut the aubergines in half lengthways and scoop out the flesh.

Heat the oil in a large, heavy-based frying pan, add the aubergine flesh and fry for 5 minutes. Put the aubergine mixture into a food processor, add the lemon juice and blend until smooth. Gradually add the yogurt, then the garlic and cumin. Season with salt and pepper.

Turn the mixture into a serving bowl and chill in the refrigerator for at least 1 hour. Garnish with chopped parsley and serve with pepper strips.

*If you prefer your garlic to have a mellower flavour, add it to the pan with the aubergine flesh and tip them both into the food processor after 5 minutes. Cooking reduces the sharpness.*

# Raitas

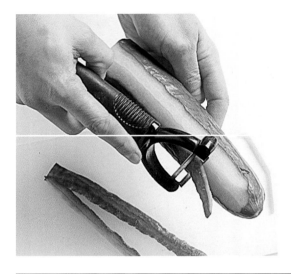
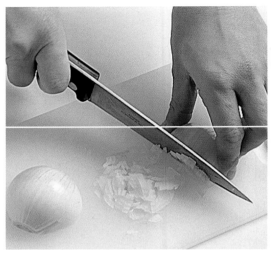

To make the mint raita, place the yogurt in a bowl and whisk with a fork. Gradually whisk in the water. Add the onion, mint sauce and salt and blend together. Garnish with mint leaves.

To make the cucumber raita, peel and slice the cucumber. Chop the onion finely. Place the cucumber and onion in a large bowl, then add the salt and the mint sauce. Add the yogurt and the water, place the mixture in a blender and blend well. Serve garnished with fresh mint leaves.

To make the aubergine raita, remove the top end of the aubergine and chop the rest into small pieces. Boil in a pan of water for 20 minutes, until softened, then drain and mash. Add the salt, onion and green chillies, mixing well. Whisk the yogurt with the water, add to the mixture and mix thoroughly.

*Raitas are easy to prepare, very versatile and have a cooling effect that will be appreciated if you are serving hot, spicy dishes.*

# Grilled Aubergine Dip

**SERVES 6–8**

1 LARGE AUBERGINE,
ABOUT 400 G/14 OZ

5 TBSP OLIVE OIL

2 SPRING ONIONS, CHOPPED
FINELY

1 LARGE GARLIC CLOVE, CRUSHED

2 TBSP FINELY CHOPPED
FRESH PARSLEY

SALT AND PEPPER

SMOKED SWEET SPANISH
PAPRIKA, TO GARNISH

FRENCH BREAD, TO SERVE

*If you are short of time, you can omit the sprinkling with salt as modern varieties of aubergine are far less bitter than those of the past. However, salting the flesh also helps to draw out moisture and prevent the aubergine from absorbing too much oil during cooking.*

Cut the aubergine into thick slices and sprinkle with salt to draw out any bitterness; set aside for 30 minutes, then rinse and pat dry.

Heat 4 tablespoons of the oil in a large frying pan over a medium-high heat. Add the aubergine slices and fry on both sides until soft and beginning to brown. Remove from the frying pan and set aside to cool. The slices will release the oil again as they cool.

Heat the remaining oil in the frying pan. Add the spring onions and garlic, and fry for 3 minutes until the spring onions become soft. Remove from the heat and set aside with the aubergine slices to cool.

Transfer all the ingredients to a food processor and process just until a coarse purée forms. Transfer to a serving bowl and stir in the parsley. Taste, and adjust the seasoning if necessary. Serve at once, or cover and chill until 15 minutes before required. Sprinkle with paprika and serve with slices of French bread.

# Pico de Gallo Salsa

SERVES 4–6

3 LARGE, RIPE TOMATOES

$^{1}/_{2}$ RED ONION, FINELY CHOPPED

1 LARGE FRESH GREEN CHILLI,
SUCH AS JALAPEÑO, DESEEDED
AND FINELY CHOPPED

2 TBSP CHOPPED FRESH
CORIANDER

JUICE OF 1 LIME, OR TO TASTE

SALT AND PEPPER

Halve the tomatoes, scoop out and discard
the seeds, and dice the flesh. Place the flesh
in a large, non-metallic bowl.

Add the onion, chilli, chopped coriander
and lime juice. Season to taste with salt and
pepper, and stir gently to combine.

Cover and leave to chill in the refrigerator
for at least 30 minutes to allow the flavours
to develop before serving.

*This is one of the most famous
Tex-Mex salsas. Its Spanish name
translates as rooster's beak, so
called, allegedly, because it
was traditionally eaten between
the thumb and forefinger,
pecking-style.*

# Coconut Sambal

**MAKES ABOUT 140 G/5 OZ**

$1/2$ FRESH COCONUT, ABOUT
115 G/4 OZ OF MEAT, OR
125 G/$4^1/2$ OZ DESICCATED
COCONUT

2 FRESH GREEN CHILLIES,
DESEEDED OR NOT, TO TASTE,
AND CHOPPED

2.5-CM/1-INCH PIECE FRESH
ROOT GINGER, FINELY CHOPPED

4 TBSP CHOPPED FRESH
CORIANDER

2 TBSP LEMON JUICE, OR TO TASTE

2 SHALLOTS, VERY FINELY
CHOPPED

*This dish is good served with
poppadoms as a snack or simply
with grilled fresh seafood.*

If you are using a whole coconut, use a hammer and nail to punch a hole in the 'eye' of the coconut, then pour out the water from the inside and reserve. Use the hammer to break the coconut in half, then peel half and chop.

Put the coconut and chillies in a small food processor and whiz for about 30 seconds until finely chopped. Add the ginger, coriander and lemon juice and whiz again.

If the mixture seems too dry, whiz in about 1 tablespoon coconut water or water. Stir in the shallots and serve immediately, or cover and chill until required. This will keep its fresh flavour, covered, in the refrigerator for up to 3 days.

# Mint and Cannellini Bean Dip

SERVES 6

175 G/6 OZ DRIED CANNELLINI
BEANS

1 SMALL GARLIC CLOVE, CRUSHED

1 BUNCH OF SPRING ONIONS,
ROUGHLY CHOPPED

HANDFUL OF FRESH MINT LEAVES

2 TBSP TAHINI

2 TBSP OLIVE OIL

1 TSP GROUND CUMIN

1 TSP GROUND CORIANDER

LEMON JUICE

SALT AND PEPPER

FRESH MINT SPRIGS, TO GARNISH

FRESH VEGETABLE CRUDITÉS,
SUCH AS CAULIFLOWER FLORETS,
CARROTS, CUCUMBER, RADISHES
AND PEPPERS, TO SERVE

*You could make this dip with
other kinds of dried beans. White
beans, kidney and navy beans
would work well but you could
also use borlotti, pinto, or
flageolet. Soak in cold water and
cook as described below until
tender – some varieties will take
longer than others. Do not add
salt when boiling any dried
beans or they will become tough.*

Put the cannellini beans into a bowl and
add sufficient cold water to cover. Set aside
to soak for at least 4 hours or overnight.

Rinse and drain the beans, put them into
a large saucepan and cover them with cold
water. Bring to the boil and boil rapidly for
10 minutes. Reduce the heat, cover and
simmer until tender.

Drain the beans thoroughly and transfer
them to a bowl or food processor. Add the
garlic, spring onions, mint, tahini and olive
oil. Process the mixture for about 15 seconds
or mash well by hand until smooth.

Scrape the mixture into a bowl, if necessary,
and stir in the cumin, coriander and lemon
juice. Season to taste with salt and pepper.
Mix thoroughly, cover with clingfilm and set
aside in a cool place, but not the refrigerator,
for 30 minutes, to allow the flavours to
develop fully.

Spoon the dip into individual serving bowls
and garnish with sprigs of mint. Place the
bowls on plates, surrounded with vegetable
crudités. Serve at room temperature.

# Savoury Sauces

Of the many recipes in this section, some, such as Classic Bolognese Meat Sauce, form an integral part of a dish, while others, such as Romesco Sauce, are designed to add that special extra touch. There are sauces for pasta, dipping, coating, pouring, and even mopping up with bread at the end of the meal because they are far too delicious to leave on the plate. They are based on a wide range of ingredients, from meat to seafood and from vegetables to eggs, and can be served with an equally extensive choice of dishes. To take just one example, Satay Sauce is great with grilled chicken, pork, beef, prawns, fish and vegetable kebabs and proves a sensational topping for boiled new potatoes. Master the art of making any of these sauces – and it isn't difficult – and you automatically expand your repertoire of starters and main course dishes.

# Classic Bolognese Meat Sauce

**SERVES 4**

2 TBSP OLIVE OIL

1 TBSP BUTTER

1 SMALL ONION, CHOPPED FINELY

1 CARROT, CHOPPED FINELY

1 CELERY STICK, CHOPPED FINELY

50 G/1¾ OZ MUSHROOMS, DICED

225 G/8 OZ MINCED BEEF

75 G/2¾ OZ UNSMOKED BACON OR HAM, DICED

2 CHICKEN LIVERS, CHOPPED

2 TBSP TOMATO PURÉE

125 ML/4 FL OZ DRY WHITE WINE

SALT AND PEPPER

½ TSP FRESHLY GRATED NUTMEG

300 ML/10 FL OZ CHICKEN STOCK

125 ML/4 FL OZ DOUBLE CREAM

450 G/1 LB DRIED SPAGHETTI

2 TBSP CHOPPED FRESH PARSLEY, TO GARNISH

FRESHLY GRATED PARMESAN CHEESE, TO SERVE

*In Bologna, the city in northern Italy where this sauce originated, it is simply called ragù and is always served with tagliatelle. Nevertheless, spaghetti bolognese has become traditional elsewhere and even though purists may not approve, the sauce goes well with any kind of pasta to which it can cling, even small shapes, such as fusilli, which children may find more appealing and easier to eat.*

Heat the oil and butter in a large saucepan over a medium heat. Add the onion, carrot, celery and mushrooms to the pan, then fry until soft. Add the beef and bacon to the pan and fry until the beef is evenly browned.

Stir in the chicken livers and tomato purée and cook for 2–3 minutes. Pour in the wine and season with salt, pepper and the nutmeg. Add the stock. Bring to the boil, then cover and simmer gently over a low heat for 1 hour. Stir in the cream and simmer, uncovered, until reduced.

Cook the pasta in plenty of boiling salted water until al dente. Drain and transfer to a warm serving dish.

Pour half the sauce over the pasta. Toss well to mix. Spoon the remaining sauce over the top.

Garnish with the parsley and serve with Parmesan cheese.

# Chicken Skewers and Satay Sauce

**CHICKEN SKEWERS**

2 TBSP VEGETABLE OR
GROUNDNUT OIL

1 TBSP SESAME OIL

JUICE OF ½ LIME

2 SKINNED, BONED CHICKEN
BREASTS, CUT INTO SMALL CUBES

**SATAY SAUCE**

2 TBSP VEGETABLE OR
GROUNDNUT OIL

1 SMALL ONION, CHOPPED FINELY

1 SMALL FRESH GREEN CHILLI,
DESEEDED AND CHOPPED

1 GARLIC CLOVE, CHOPPED FINELY

125 ML/4 FL OZ CRUNCHY
PEANUT BUTTER

6–8 TBSP WATER

JUICE OF ½ LIME

For the chicken skewers, combine both the oils and the lime juice in a non-metallic dish. Add the chicken cubes, cover with clingfilm and chill for 1 hour.

To make the satay sauce, heat the oil in a frying pan and fry the onion, chilli and garlic over a low heat, stirring occasionally, for about 5 minutes, until just softened. Add the peanut butter, water and lime juice, and simmer gently, stirring constantly, until the peanut butter has softened enough to make a dip – you may need to add extra water to make a thinner consistency.

Meanwhile, drain the chicken cubes and thread them on to 8–12 wooden skewers. Put under a hot grill or on a barbecue, turning frequently, for about 10 minutes, until cooked and browned. Serve hot with the warm sauce.

*These chicken skewers taste great cooked under the grill, but using the barbecue adds that extra smoky flavour.*

# Pesto Genovese

**MAKES ABOUT 225 ML/8 FL OZ**

2 GARLIC CLOVES, COARSELY CHOPPED

25 G/1 OZ PINE NUTS

40 G/1½ OZ FRESH BASIL LEAVES

1 TSP COARSE SALT

25 G/1 OZ FRESHLY GRATED PARMESAN CHEESE

125–150 ML/4–5 FL OZ EXTRA-VIRGIN OLIVE OIL

Put the garlic, pine nuts, basil leaves and salt into a blender and process to a purée. Add the Parmesan and process briefly again. You can do this by hand using a pestle and mortar.

Then add 125 ml/4 fl oz oil and process again. If the consistency is too thick, add the remaining oil and process again until smooth.

*Pesto was invented in the Italian port of Genoa, where its citizens claim to grow the best basil in the world. Nowadays, pesto – often served with hot pasta – is made with a wide variety of different herbs such as parsley, mint or arugula (rocket), and even sun-dried tomatoes in oil can be substituted for the basil. Try using hazelnuts or walnuts instead of pine nuts for a change of flavour.*

# Romesco Sauce

MAKES ABOUT 300 ML/10 FL OZ

4 LARGE, RIPE TOMATOES

16 BLANCHED ALMONDS

3 LARGE GARLIC CLOVES, UNPEELED AND LEFT WHOLE

1 DRIED SWEET CHILLI, SUCH AS ÑORA, SOAKED FOR 20 MINUTES AND PATTED DRY

4 DRIED RED CHILLIES, SOAKED FOR 20 MINUTES AND PATTED DRY

PINCH OF SUGAR

150 ML/¼ PINT EXTRA-VIRGIN OLIVE OIL

ABOUT 2 TBSP RED WINE VINEGAR

SALT AND PEPPER

*This tomato sauce is traditionally served with fish and shellfish but is ideal for adding instant flavour to simply cooked chicken, pork or lamb. Authentic recipes are made with dried romesco chillies, which have a sweet and hot flavour. Unfortunately they are quite hard to obtain, so this recipe uses dried ñora chilli.*

Place the tomatoes, almonds and garlic on a baking sheet and roast in a preheated oven, 180°C/350°F/Gas Mark 4, for 20 minutes, but check the almonds after about 7 minutes, because they can burn quickly; remove as soon as they are golden and start to give off an aroma.

Peel the roasted garlic and tomatoes. Put the almonds, garlic, sweet chilli and dried red chillies in a food processor and process until finely chopped. Add the tomatoes and sugar and process again.

With the motor running, slowly add the olive oil through the feed tube. Add 1½ tablespoons of the vinegar and quickly process. Taste and add extra vinegar, if desired, and salt and pepper to taste.

Leave to stand for at least 2 hours, then serve at room temperature. Alternatively, cover and chill for up to 3 days, then bring to room temperature before serving. Stir in any oil that separates before serving.

# Traditional Gravy Recipes

SERVES 4

**CHICKEN GRAVY**

1 TBSP CORNFLOUR

2 TBSP WATER

CHICKEN JUICES FROM
A CHICKEN ROASTING TIN

SALT AND PEPPER

**BEEF GRAVY**

MEAT JUICES FROM
THE ROASTING TIN

3 TBSP FLOUR

300 ML/10 FL OZ RED WINE

300 ML/10 FL OZ BEEF STOCK

2 TBSP WORCESTERSHIRE SAUCE
(OPTIONAL)

SALT AND PEPPER

**ONION GRAVY**

2 TBSP SUNFLOWER OIL

1 ONION, CHOPPED

1 TBSP PLAIN FLOUR

200 ML/7 FL OZ CHICKEN STOCK

1 TSP RED WINE VINEGAR

SALT AND PEPPER

*For a vegetarian onion gravy, substitute the chicken stock with vegetable stock.*

For the chicken gravy, blend the cornflour with the water, then stir into the juices in the roasting tin. Transfer to the hob. Stir over a low heat until thickened. Add more water to the gravy, if necessary. Season to taste with salt and pepper.

To make the beef gravy, pour off most of the fat from the tin, leaving behind the meat juices and the sediment. Place the tin on the hob over a medium heat and scrape all the sediment from the base of the tin. Sprinkle in the flour and quickly mix it into the juices with a small whisk. When you have a smooth paste, gradually add the wine and most of the stock, whisking constantly. Bring to the boil, then reduce the heat to a gentle simmer and cook for 2–3 minutes. Season to taste with salt and pepper and add the remaining stock, if needed, and a little Worcestershire sauce, if you like.

For the onion gravy, heat the oil in a large saucepan, add the onion and cook over a low heat, stirring occasionally, for 5 minutes, or until softened. Sprinkle in the flour and cook, stirring, for 1 minute. Remove the saucepan from the heat and gradually stir in the chicken stock. Return to the heat and gradually bring to the boil, stirring constantly. Stir in the vinegar and season to taste with salt and pepper.

# Fish Cakes and Thai Dipping Sauce

SERVES 4

### FISH CAKES

450 G/1 LB WHITE FISH FILLETS, SKINNED AND CUT INTO CUBES

1 EGG WHITE

2 KAFFIR LIME LEAVES, TORN COARSELY

1 TBSP GREEN CURRY PASTE

55 G/2 OZ FRENCH BEANS, CHOPPED FINELY

1 FRESH RED CHILLI, DESEEDED AND CHOPPED FINELY

BUNCH OF FRESH CORIANDER, CHOPPED

VEGETABLE OR GROUNDNUT OIL FOR FRYING

### DIPPING SAUCE

115 G/4 OZ CASTER SUGAR

50 ML/2 FL OZ WHITE WINE VINEGAR

1 SMALL CARROT, CUT INTO THIN BATONS

5-CM/2-INCH PIECE CUCUMBER, PEELED, DESEEDED AND CUT INTO THIN BATONS

*Dipping sauces are hugely popular in Thailand and this one can be served with a wide variety of dishes and tasty morsels, including pancake rolls, deep-fried crab claws, wonton pouches, rice cakes, and miniature meatballs. If you like, you can substitute rice vinegar for the white wine vinegar and add a pinch of chopped fresh or crushed dried chilli.*

Put the fish into a food processor with the egg white, lime leaves and curry paste, and process until smooth. Scrape the mixture into a bowl and stir in the French beans, red chilli and coriander.

With dampened hands, shape the mixture into small patties, about 5 cm/2 inches across. Place them on a large plate in a single layer and chill for 30 minutes.

Meanwhile, make the dipping sauce. Put the sugar in a saucepan with 1$\frac{1}{2}$ tablespoons water and the vinegar, and heat gently, stirring until the sugar has dissolved. Add the carrot and cucumber, then remove from the heat and leave to cool.

Heat the oil in a frying pan and fry the fish cakes, in batches, until golden brown on both sides. Drain on kitchen paper and keep warm while you cook the remaining batches. If you like, reheat the dipping sauce. Serve the fish cakes immediately with warm or cold dipping sauce.

# Hot Sauce of Dried Chillies

**MAKES ABOUT 225 ML/8 FL OZ**

10 DRIED ARBOL CHILLIES,
STEMS REMOVED

225 ML/8 FL OZ CIDER
OR WHITE WINE VINEGAR

$1/2$ TSP SALT

Place the dried arbol chillies in a mortar and crush finely with a pestle.

Put the cider or white wine vinegar in a pan and add the crushed chillies and salt. Stir to combine, then bring the liquid to the boil.

Remove from the heat and set aside to cool completely to let the flavours infuse. Pour into a bowl and serve. The sauce will keep for up to a month, if covered and kept in the refrigerator.

*Arbol are dried, long, hot red chillies, with a dusty heat that is reminiscent of the Mexican desert. If arbol chillies are not available, use hot dried chilli or chilli flakes, such as cayenne.*

# Spareribs and Sweet-and-Sour Sauce

SERVES 4

450 G/1 LB SPARERIBS, CUT
INTO BITE-SIZED PIECES

VEGETABLE OR GROUNDNUT OIL,
FOR DEEP-FRYING

**MARINADE**

2 TSP LIGHT SOY SAUCE

1/2 TSP SALT

PINCH OF WHITE PEPPER

**SWEET-AND-SOUR SAUCE**

3 TBSP WHITE RICE VINEGAR

2 TBSP SUGAR

1 TBSP LIGHT SOY SAUCE

1 TBSP TOMATO KETCHUP

1 1/2 TBSP VEGETABLE OR
GROUNDNUT OIL

1 GREEN PEPPER, ROUGHLY
CHOPPED

1 SMALL ONION, ROUGHLY
CHOPPED

1 SMALL CARROT, FINELY SLICED

1/2 TSP FINELY CHOPPED GARLIC

1/2 TSP FINELY CHOPPED GINGER

100 G/3 1/2 OZ PINEAPPLE CHUNKS

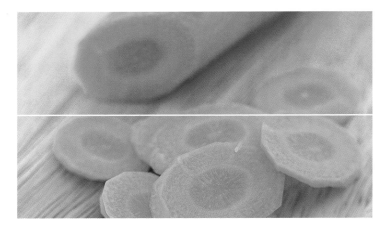

*The original sweet-and-sour sauce, on which this version is based, is often associated with fish. This variation, incorporating tomato ketchup and pineapple chunks, is matched with pork.*

Combine the marinade ingredients in a bowl with the pork and marinate for at least 20 minutes.

Heat enough oil for deep-frying in a wok, deep-fat fryer or large heavy-based saucepan until it reaches 180–190°C/350–375°F, or until a cube of bread browns in 30 seconds. Deep-fry the spareribs for 8 minutes. Drain and set aside.

To prepare the sauce, first mix together the vinegar, sugar, light soy sauce and ketchup. Set aside.

In a preheated wok or deep pan, heat 1 tablespoon of the oil and stir-fry the pepper, onion and carrot for 2 minutes. Remove and set aside.

In the clean preheated wok or deep frying pan, heat the remaining oil and stir-fry the garlic and ginger until fragrant. Add the vinegar mixture. Bring back to the boil and add the pineapple chunks. Finally, add the spareribs and the pepper, onion and carrot. Stir until warmed through and serve immediately.

# Smoked Salmon, Soured Cream and Mustard Sauce

**SERVES 4**

450 G/1 LB TAGLIATELLE
OR CONCHIGLIE

300 ML/10 FL OZ SOURED CREAM

2 TSP DIJON MUSTARD

4 LARGE SPRING ONIONS,
SLICED FINELY

225 G/8 OZ SMOKED SALMON,
CUT INTO BITE-SIZED PIECES

FINELY GRATED PEEL OF 1/2 LEMON

PEPPER

2 TBSP CHOPPED FRESH CHIVES

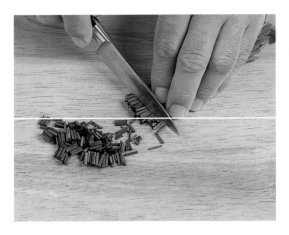 

Cook the pasta in plenty of boiling salted water until al dente. Drain and return to the pan. Add the soured cream, mustard, spring onions, smoked salmon and lemon peel to the pasta.

Stir over a low heat until heated through. Season with pepper.

Transfer to a serving dish. Sprinkle with the chives. Serve warm or at room temperature.

*Once an expensive luxury, smoked salmon is now more affordable as a result of fish farming. Even so, it is still something of a special treat. Some supermarkets and delicatessens sell inexpensive trimmings, the slightly misshapen pieces left over after the salmon has been sliced. These taste just as good and, as the fish needs to be cut into bite-sized pieces, will not affect the appearance.*

# Asparagus with Hollandaise Sauce

**SERVES 4**

650 G/1 LB 7 OZ WHITE
OR GREEN ASPARAGUS

**HOLLANDAISE SAUCE**

4 TBSP WHITE WINE VINEGAR

1/2 TBSP FINELY CHOPPED SHALLOT

5 BLACK PEPPERCORNS

1 BAY LEAF

3 LARGE EGG YOLKS

140 G/5 OZ UNSALTED BUTTER,
FINELY DICED

2 TSP LEMON JUICE

PINCH OF CAYENNE PEPPER

2 TBSP SINGLE CREAM (OPTIONAL)

SALT

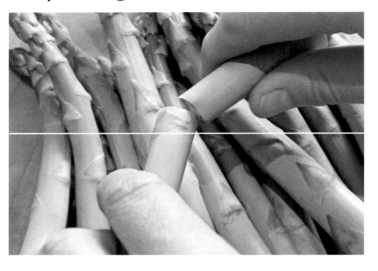

*In France, the whole country celebrates when asparagus comes into season in April. It features on menus du jour in everything from small cafés to Michelin-starred restaurants, and is often served with a Hollandaise sauce. You'll find it piled high on market stalls and on stalls at farm gates.*

Whether you are using white or green asparagus, break off any woody ends of the stems. Trim the stalks so that they are all the same height. Use a small knife to remove the stringy fibres from the white asparagus, trimming from the tip towards the end.

Bring a kettle of water to the boil. Divide the asparagus into 4 bundles and tie together with kitchen string, criss-crossing the string from just below the tips to the base.

Stand the bundles upright in a deep saucepan. Pour in enough boiling water to come about three-quarters of the way up the stalks and then cover them with a loose tent of foil, shiny-side down, inside the pan. Heat the water in the saucepan until bubbles appear around the side of the pan, then continue simmering for 10 minutes, or until the stalks are just tender when pierced with the tip of a knife.

To make the Hollandaise sauce, put the vinegar, shallot, peppercorns and bay leaf in a small saucepan over a high heat and boil until reduced to 1 tablespoon. Leave to cool slightly, then strain into a heatproof bowl that will fit over a saucepan of simmering water without the bowl touching the water.

Beat the egg yolks into the vinegar mixture. Set the bowl over the saucepan of simmering water and whisk the egg yolks constantly until they are thick enough to leave a trail on the surface. Do not let the water boil. Gradually beat in the butter, piece by piece, whisking constantly until the sauce is like soft mayonnaise. Stir in the lemon juice, then add salt to taste and the cayenne pepper. Stir in the cream for a richer taste, if desired.

Transfer to 4 small serving bowls. Drain the asparagus. Untie the bundles and arrange the spears on individual plates. Serve immediately with the Hollandaise Sauce.

# Tomato and Red Pepper Sauce

**MAKES ABOUT 700 ML/1¼ PINTS**

4 TBSP OLIVE OIL

10 LARGE GARLIC CLOVES

140 G/5 OZ SHALLOTS, CHOPPED

4 LARGE RED PEPPERS, CORED, DESEEDED AND CHOPPED

1 KG/2 LB 4 OZ GOOD-FLAVOURED RIPE, FRESH TOMATOES, CHOPPED, OR 1.2 KG/2LB 12 OZ GOOD-QUALITY CANNED CHOPPED TOMATOES

2 THIN STRIPS FRESHLY PARED ORANGE RIND

PINCH HOT RED PEPPER FLAKES (OPTIONAL), TO TASTE

SALT AND PEPPER

*You can alter the amount of orange rind you add to this simple, all-purpose sauce and really change its character. Large strips of rind, for example, lift the flavours in winter when fresh tomatoes can be insipid.*

Heat the olive oil in a large, flameproof casserole over a medium heat. Add the garlic, shallots and peppers, and fry for about 10 minutes, stirring occasionally, until the peppers are soft, but not brown.

Add the tomatoes, including the juices if using canned ones, orange rind, hot pepper flakes, if using, and salt and pepper to taste, and bring to the boil. Reduce the heat to as low as possible and simmer, uncovered, for 45 minutes, or until the liquid evaporates and the sauce thickens.

Purée the sauce through a mouli, or in a food processor, then use a wooden spoon to press through a fine sieve. Taste and adjust the seasoning if necessary. Use at once, or cover and chill for up to 3 days.

# Wrinkled Potatoes with Mojo Sauce

SERVES 4–6

70 G/2½ OZ SEA SALT

24 SMALL, NEW RED-SKINNED POTATOES, UNPEELED AND KEPT WHOLE

*MOJO SAUCE*

40 G/1½ OZ DAY-OLD BREAD, CRUSTS REMOVED AND TORN INTO SMALL PIECES

2 LARGE GARLIC CLOVES

½ TSP SALT

1½ TBSP HOT SPANISH PAPRIKA

1 TBSP GROUND CUMIN

APPROXIMATELY 2 TBSP RED WINE VINEGAR

APPROXIMATELY 5 TBSP EXTRA-VIRGIN OLIVE OIL

2 PIMIENTOS DEL PIQUILLO, PRESERVED, DRAINED AND CHOPPED

*Have plenty of cold beers or water on hand when you serve this classic Spanish tapas dish. The potatoes are cooked in heavily salted water that resembles seawater, resulting in a thin film of salt on the skins. The salt and piquant sauce can make you very thirsty.*

Pour about 2.5 cm/1 inch water into a saucepan and stir in the sea salt. Add the potatoes and stir again; they do not have to be covered with water. Fold a clean tea towel to fit over the potatoes, then bring the water to the boil. Reduce the heat and simmer for 20 minutes, or until the potatoes are tender, but still holding together.

Remove the tea towel and set aside. Drain the potatoes and return them to the empty saucepan. When the tea towel is cool enough to handle, wring the saltwater it contains into the saucepan. Put the saucepan over a low heat and shake until the potatoes are dry and coated with a thin white film. Remove from the heat.

Meanwhile, make the Mojo Sauce. Put the bread in a bowl and add just enough water to cover, set aside for 5 minutes to soften. Use your hands to squeeze all the water from the bread. Use a pestle and mortar to mash the garlic and salt into a paste. Stir in the paprika and cumin. Transfer the mixture to a food processor. Add 2 tablespoons of vinegar and blend, then add the bread and 2 tablespoons of oil and blend again.

With the motor running, add the pepper pieces to the food processor a few at a time until they are puréed and a sauce forms. Add more oil, if necessary, until the sauce is smooth and thick. Taste and adjust the seasoning, adding extra vinegar, if necessary.

To serve, cut the potatoes in half and spear with wooden cocktail sticks. Serve with a bowl of sauce on the side for dipping. The potatoes can be eaten hot or at room temperature.

# Prawn and Garlic Sauce with Cream

**SERVES 4**

3 TBSP OLIVE OIL

3 TBSP BUTTER

4 GARLIC CLOVES, CHOPPED
VERY FINELY

2 TBSP FINELY DICED RED PEPPER

2 TBSP TOMATO PURÉE

125 ML/4 FL OZ DRY WHITE WINE

450 G/1 LB TAGLIATELLE
OR SPAGHETTI

350 G/12 OZ RAW PRAWNS,
PEELED AND DEVEINED, CUT INTO
1–CM/1/2–INCH PIECES

125 ML/4 FL OZ DOUBLE CREAM

SALT AND PEPPER

3 TBSP CHOPPED FRESH
FLAT-LEAF PARSLEY, TO GARNISH

Heat the oil and butter in a saucepan over a medium-low heat. Add the garlic and red pepper. Fry for a few seconds until the garlic is just beginning to colour. Stir in the tomato purée and wine. Cook for 10 minutes, stirring.

Cook the pasta in plenty of boiling salted water until al dente. Drain the pasta and return to the pan.

Add the prawns to the sauce and raise the heat to medium-high. Cook for 2 minutes, stirring, until the prawns turn pink. Reduce the heat and stir in the cream. Cook for 1 minute, stirring constantly, until thickened. Season with salt and pepper.

Transfer the pasta to a warm serving dish. Pour the sauce over the pasta. Sprinkle with the parsley. Toss well to mix and serve at once.

*It is best to remove the black vein that runs along the back of the prawn. To do this, make a shallow cut with a sharp knife along the length of the peeled prawn and remove the vein with the tip of the knife or the point of a toothpick. While it is not toxic, the thread-like vein can adversely affect the flavour of the dish.*

# Essential Recipes

In this section you will find the most useful sauces and dressings for all occasions. For those of us who have become used to buying many of these basics at the supermarket, tasting the home-made versions for the first time is likely to prove a revelation. For a start, using fresh ingredients makes a huge difference and the absence of any artificial additives is reassuring for the health-conscious. Also, it's simple to make slight adjustments so that the flavour and texture are precisely to your liking – a sharper or mellower Vinaigrette, for example. Many of these recipes are immensely versatile and form the basis of a wide variety of other sauces and dressings, which simply require the addition of an extra ingredient or two, whether fresh herbs or chopped anchovy fillets. Finally, the recipe for Mayonnaise should at last dispel the misbegotten notion that there is something incredibly difficult about making this useful, popular – and easy – cold sauce.

# Sweet-and-Sour Dressing

**SERVES 2–4**

2 TBSP LEMON JUICE, OR RED
OR WHITE WINE VINEGAR

4–6 TBSP EXTRA-VIRGIN OLIVE OIL

1 TBSP HONEY

1 TSP DIJON MUSTARD

1 TSP FINELY GRATED
ROOT GINGER

PINCH OF CASTER SUGAR

1 TBSP FRESHLY CHOPPED
PARSLEY

SALT AND PEPPER

*A basic dressing is essential for a good salad. Good olive oil and a fine vinegar or lemon juice should be used. Vary the oil and vinegar according to the salad ingredients and add appropriate herbs at the last minute. Salads should only be dressed immediately before eating, or the leaves will go soggy. For the simplest dressing, just sprinkle over some freshly squeezed lemon juice and some olive oil.*

Place all the ingredients in a jar, secure the top and shake well. Alternatively, beat all the ingredients together in a small basin. Use as much oil as you like. If you have just salad leaves to dress, then 4 tablespoons of oil will be sufficient, but if you have heavier ingredients like potatoes, you will need 6 tablespoons of oil.

Use the dressing at once. If you want to store it, do not add the herbs – it will then keep for 3–4 days in the refrigerator.

## Variation

**Asian dressing:** Replace 1 tablespoon of the oil with sesame oil and replace the honey and root ginger with 1–2 teaspoons of soy sauce. Add chopped coriander instead of the parsley.

# Vinaigrette

125 ML/4 FL OZ OLIVE
OR OTHER VEGETABLE OIL

3 TBSP WHITE WINE VINEGAR
OR LEMON JUICE

1 TSP DIJON MUSTARD

1/2 TSP CASTER SUGAR

SALT AND PEPPER

*A vinaigrette is a great way to capture the flavour of simple salads, but with so few ingredients, it is essential to use good-quality oil and vinegar.*

Put all the ingredients in a jar then, using a stick blender, blend until a thick emulsion forms. Alternatively, put all the ingredients in a screw-top jar, secure the lid and shake vigorously until the emulsion forms. Taste and adjust the seasoning if necessary.

Use the vinaigrette at once or store in an airtight container in the refrigerator for up to a month. Always whisk or shake the dressing again before using.

## Variations

**Garlic Vinaigrette:** Use a good-quality garlic-flavoured oil and add 1 or 2 crushed garlic cloves to taste. The longer the garlic cloves are left in the dressing, the more pronounced the flavour will be – they should be removed after a week.

**Herb Vinaigrette:** Stir 1 1/2 tablespoons chopped fresh herbs, such as chives, parsley, or mint, or a mixture, into the basic vinaigrette. Use within 3 days and strain through a fine non-metallic strainer if the herbs begin to darken.

# Mayonnaise

MAKES ABOUT 300 ML/10 FL OZ

2 LARGE EGG YOLKS

2 TSP DIJON MUSTARD

¾ TSP SALT, OR TO TASTE

WHITE PEPPER

2 TBSP LEMON JUICE
OR WHITE WINE VINEGAR

ABOUT 300 ML/10 FL OZ
SUNFLOWER OIL

Whiz the egg yolks with the Dijon mustard, salt and white pepper to taste in a food processor, blender or by hand. Add the lemon juice and whiz again.

With the motor still running or still beating, add the oil, drop by drop at first. When the sauce begins to thicken, the oil can then be added in a slow, steady stream. Taste and adjust the seasoning with extra salt, pepper and lemon juice if necessary. If the sauce seems too thick, slowly add 1 tablespoon hot water, single cream or lemon juice.

Use at once or store in an airtight container in the refrigerator for up to 1 week.

*One of the basic sauces in the French repertoire, home-made mayonnaise has a milder flavour than most commercial varieties. Because this recipe uses raw egg yolks, it should be avoided by infants, the elderly, pregnant women, convalescents and anyone suffering from an illness.*

# Mango Chutney

MAKES ABOUT 250 G/9 OZ

1 LARGE MANGO, ABOUT
400 G/14 OZ, PEELED,
STONED AND FINELY CHOPPED

2 TBSP LIME JUICE

1 TBSP VEGETABLE OR
GROUNDNUT OIL

2 SHALLOTS, FINELY CHOPPED

1 GARLIC CLOVE, FINELY CHOPPED

2 FRESH GREEN CHILLIES,
DESEEDED AND FINELY SLICED

1 TSP BLACK MUSTARD SEEDS

1 TSP CORIANDER SEEDS

5 TBSP GRATED JAGGERY SUGAR
OR LIGHT BROWN SUGAR

5 TBSP WHITE WINE VINEGAR

1 TSP SALT

PINCH OF GROUND GINGER

*This light, spiced chutney is about as far as one can get from the thick, overly sweet mango chutney that can be bought in jars. It adds a sunny flavour to any meal.*

Put the mango in a non-metallic bowl with the lime juice and set aside.

Heat the oil in a large frying pan or saucepan over a medium-high heat. Add the shallots and fry for 3 minutes. Add the garlic and chillies and stir for a further 2 minutes, or until the shallots are soft, but not brown. Add the mustard and coriander seeds and then stir around.

Add the mango to the pan with the jaggery, vinegar, salt and ground ginger and stir around. Reduce the heat to its lowest setting and simmer for 10 minutes until the liquid thickens and the mango becomes sticky.

Remove from the heat and leave to cool completely. Transfer to an airtight container, cover and chill for 3 days before using. Store in the refrigerator and use within 1 week.

# Bread and Cranberry Sauces

SERVES 6–8

**BREAD SAUCE**

1 ONION

12 CLOVES

1 BAY LEAF

6 BLACK PEPPERCORNS

600 ML/1 PINT MILK

115 G/4 OZ FRESH WHITE BREADCRUMBS

2 TBSP BUTTER

WHOLE NUTMEG, FOR GRATING

2 TBSP DOUBLE CREAM, OPTIONAL

SALT AND PEPPER

**CRANBERRY SAUCE**

25 G/8 OZ FRESH CRANBERRIES

85 G/3 OZ SOFT BROWN SUGAR

150 ML/5 FL OZ ORANGE JUICE

1/2 TSP GROUND CINNAMON

1/2 TSP GRATED NUTMEG

*Bread Sauce is a traditional accompaniment to turkey for Christmas, but is also very useful for serving with cold meats, such as chicken or ham.*

To make the Bread Sauce, make small holes in the onion using the point of a sharp knife or a skewer, and stick the cloves in them. Put the onion, bay leaf and peppercorns in a saucepan and pour in the milk. Bring to the boil, then remove from the heat, cover, and leave to infuse for 1 hour.

Discard the onion and bay leaf, and sieve the milk to remove the peppercorns. Return the milk to the cleaned saucepan and add the breadcrumbs.

Cook the sauce over a very low heat for 4–5 minutes, until the breadcrumbs have swollen and the sauce is thick.

Beat in the butter and season well with salt and pepper, and a good grating of nutmeg. Stir in the cream just before serving, if using.

To make the Cranberry Sauce, place the cranberries, sugar, orange juice and spices in a saucepan and stir well. Cover the saucepan and bring slowly to the boil over a gentle heat.

Simmer for 8–10 minutes, or until the cranberries have burst. Take care because they may splash.

Put the sauce in a serving bowl and cover until needed. Serve warm or cold.

# Apricot, Mint and Quick Horseradish Sauces

**APRICOT SAUCE**

400 G/14 OZ CANNED APRICOT HALVES IN SYRUP

150 ML/5 FL OZ VEGETABLE STOCK (MADE FROM POWDER)

125 ML/4 FL OZ MARSALA WINE

1/2 TSP GROUND GINGER

1/2 TSP GROUND CINNAMON

SALT AND PEPPER

**QUICK HORSERADISH SAUCE**

6 TBSP CREAMED HORSERADISH SAUCE

6 TBSP CRÈME FRAÎCHE

**MINT SAUCE**

SMALL BUNCH FRESH MINT LEAVES

2 TSP CASTER SUGAR

2 TBSP BOILING WATER

2 TBSP WHITE WINE VINEGAR

*The recipe listed here for Mint Sauce is a simple classic – you can vary it by experimenting with different vinegars, for example malt vinegar, cider vinegar, or tarragon wine vinegar, among others. Mint Sauce is so versatile, you can even add extra ingredients such as honey.*

For the Apricot Sauce, put the canned apricots and syrup into a blender and blend until smooth.

Pour the pureé into a saucepan, add the other ingredients and mix well. Heat the sauce gently over a low heat for about 4–5 minutes until warm. Season to taste.

Remove from the heat and pour the sauce into a serving jug. This sauce is a good accompaniment to gammon.

For the Quick Horseradish Sauce, mix the horseradish and crème fraîche together in a small serving bowl. Serve the sauce with roast beef or smoked fish such as trout or mackerel.

For the Mint Sauce, make sure the mint is clean and tear the leaves from their stems. If the mint is dirty, wash it gently and dry thoroughly before tearing.

Place the leaves on a chopping board and sprinkle with the sugar. Chop the leaves finely (the sugar helps the chopping process) and place in a small bowl. Pour over the boiling water and stir to dissolve the sugar.

Add the vinegar and leave to stand for 30 minutes. This sauce goes particularly well with roast lamb.

# Sweet Sauces

Sometimes, especially for everyday family meals, it can be hard to find the time to create a special dessert. The sweet sauces in this section provide an easy way to turn a simple dessert into a triumphant finale to family supper. All of them, hot and cold, will transform a scoop of ready-made ice cream, but they also go well with a huge range of other sweet treats, from steamed puddings to pancakes and from flans to mousses. Just because they're easy to make doesn't mean that they aren't good enough to serve to guests – any of the Ice Cream Sauces would go beautifully with a meringue gateau and White Chocolate Fudge Sauce is just perfect for a fruit-packed, nut-sprinkled ice cream sundae. And why not try a fresh fruit fondue with French Chocolate Sauce for a fabulous end to an al fresco meal.

# White Chocolate Fudge Sauce

150 ML/5 FL OZ DOUBLE CREAM

4 TBSP UNSALTED BUTTER,
CUT INTO SMALL PIECES

3 TBSP CASTER SUGAR

175 G/6 OZ WHITE CHOCOLATE,
BROKEN INTO PIECES

2 TBSP BRANDY

Pour the cream into the top of a double boiler or a heatproof bowl set over a saucepan of gently simmering water. Add the butter and sugar and stir until the mixture is smooth. Remove from the heat.

Stir in the chocolate, a few pieces at a time, waiting until each batch has melted before adding the next. Add the brandy and stir the sauce until smooth. Cool to room temperature before serving.

*This creamy white chocolate sauce adds a touch of sophistication and luxury to the dinner table.*

# French Chocolate Sauce

**MAKES 150 ML/5 FL OZ**

6 TBSP DOUBLE CREAM

85 G/3 OZ DARK CHOCOLATE,
BROKEN INTO SMALL PIECES

2 TBSP ORANGE LIQUEUR

Bring the cream gently to the boil in a small, heavy-based saucepan over a low heat. Remove the saucepan from the heat, add the broken chocolate and stir until smooth.

Stir in the liqueur and serve immediately, or keep the sauce warm until required.

*This rich, warm and alcoholic sauce is superb with both hot and cold desserts and positively magical with ice cream.*

# Berry, Chocolate and Port Sauces

*BERRY SAUCE*

225 G/8 OZ BERRIES, SUCH AS
BLACKBERRIES OR RASPBERRIES

2 TBSP WATER

2–3 TBSP CASTER SUGAR

2 TBSP FRUIT LIQUEUR, SUCH
AS CRÈME DE CASSIS OR
CRÈME DE FRAMBOISE

*CHOCOLATE SAUCE*

150 ML/5 FL OZ DOUBLE CREAM

4 TBSP UNSALTED BUTTER

55 G/2 OZ SOFT LIGHT
BROWN SUGAR

175 G/6 OZ PLAIN CHOCOLATE,
BROKEN INTO PIECES

2 TBSP DARK RUM (OPTIONAL)

*PORT SAUCE*

350 ML/12 FL OZ RUBY PORT

2 TSP CORNFLOUR

*Serve plain or chocolate ice cream with one or more of these delicious sauces on the side.*

For the Berry Sauce, put all the ingredients into a small, heavy-based saucepan and heat gently, until the sugar has dissolved and the fruit juices run. Purée with a hand-held blender or in a food processor, then push through a sieve into a serving bowl to remove the seeds. Add more sugar if necessary and serve warm or cold.

For the Chocolate Sauce, pour the cream into a heatproof bowl and add the butter and sugar. Set over a saucepan of gently simmering water and cook, stirring constantly, until smooth. Remove from the heat and set aside to cool slightly. Stir in the chocolate and continue stirring until it has melted. Stir in the rum (if using), then leave the sauce to cool to room temperature before serving.

For the Port Sauce, combine 4 tablespoons of the port with the cornflour to make a smooth paste. Pour the remainder of the port into a saucepan and bring to the boil. Stir in the cornflour paste and cook, stirring constantly, for about 1 minute, until thickened. Remove from the heat and set aside to cool. Pour the sauce into a bowl, cover and chill in the refrigerator.

# Index